SOUTHCOATES PRIMARY SCHOOL
SOUTHCOATES LANE
HULL
HU9 3TW

A Day in the Life of a...

Bus Driver

Carol Watson

FRANKLIN WATTS
LONDON • NEW YORK • SYDNEY

Winston is a bus driver.
He starts his day by checking in at the bus garage where he will begin his route.

First Winston signs on by swiping his identity card through a machine.
Then he opens up his locker to get out his equipment.

A bus driver needs a cash tray for the fares he collects, an emergency ticket pack, a fare chart and a module for the bus's ticket machine.

Winston slots his module
into the ticket machine on the bus.
This records all the fares that
he takes and adds up how much
money Winston has collected.

Next Winston sets the destination blind to show where the bus is going. Then he carries out a pre-start vehicle check.

"This headlight needs changing," he tells John, the engineer. John fixes it straightaway.

Now Winston is ready to set out on his route.

The bus stops for lots of passengers. At one stop Ben and his sister Ellie get on. "We're going to the park to sail my boat," Ben tells Winston.

"That will be eighty pence," says Winston. He gives Ben and Ellie their tickets and change, and they find a seat.

Winston makes more stops and the bus starts to fill up with passengers.

Mrs Murray is struggling to lift her shopping on to the bus.

"Let me help you," says Winston. He climbs out of his seat and helps the lady with her bags. "Thank you," says Mrs Murray.

The bus is quite crowded now and there is nowhere for the lady to sit. "Would you like my seat?" asks Ben. He stands up so that Mrs Murray can sit down.

"It's our stop next, Ellie," says Ben. "I'll press the bell." The bell rings to let Winston know that passengers want him to stop.

Ben and Ellie climb off the bus, the door closes and Winston drives away.

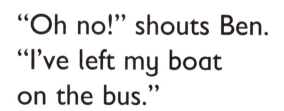

"Oh no!" shouts Ben. "I've left my boat on the bus."

At the terminus Winston checks the bus for lost property. "Oh dear," he says to himself, "the boy left his boat behind. He will be upset."

Winston takes the boat to the Lost Property Office at the garage.

Now it is time for his meal break. In the canteen Winston checks over the route for the other 'half' of his day.

Next Winston is going to drive a different bus. He takes over from Millie who has been driving it all morning. "The traffic's not too bad," she tells him.

At the end of his day Winston returns to the bus garage. A machine prints the amount of money he has collected and gives him a driver's receipt.

Winston puts the money in a counting machine.

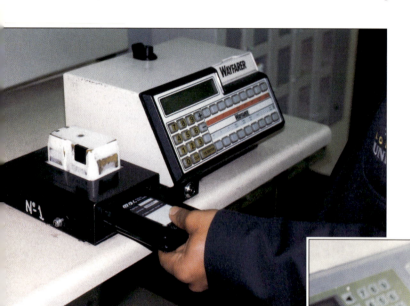

He sees Ben at the Lost Property Office. "Thank you for looking after my boat," says Ben.

Winston smiles and waves. Then he sets off for home.

Plan your own bus route

Make a plan of the bus route from your house to school, or your favourite shop. Mark on it all the bus stops that you pass along the way.

- Who else lives along the route?
- Which shops do you pass?
- Is there a church, library or anything else of interest along the way?

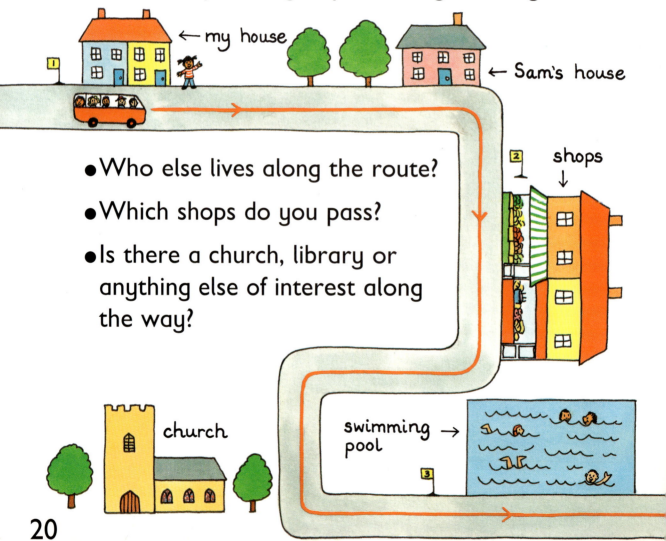

- How much is the fare from your house to school?
- What coins do you need to have for the exact fare?
- Find out the fares for other stops along the route.
- Mark them on your map.

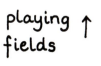
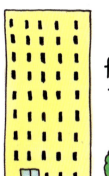

How you can help bus drivers

1. Try to have the correct money ready before you get on the bus.

2. Don't put your feet on the seats.

3. Give up your seat if an elderly person or a pregnant woman has nowhere to sit.

4. Chat quietly to your friends – rowdy behaviour is a nuisance to the driver and the other passengers.

5. If you have a bus pass make sure the details are clearly visible.

6. Check you have all your belongings before you leave the bus.

7. If you know where you are going to get off, press the bell well before the stop.

Facts about bus drivers

- To be a bus driver you need to have a driving licence. Then you apply to the Recruitment Department of your local bus company.

- An instructor from the company tests new drivers' skills by watching how they drive in a van. If they are successful they take a written test and have an interview.

- If they pass these stages a doctor examines the new drivers to see if they are fit and well. Then they can begin training.

- After about 2-3 weeks, trainee bus drivers should be ready to take the Public Carriage Vehicle driving test. If they pass the test they are sent to the garage at which they will work.

- At that garage a new driver is trained to drive all the different kinds of buses and routes that are used there. Then the bus driver begins work.

- Winston, the bus driver in this book, works in a busy city. His day is made up of two 'halves'. In each half he makes four journeys. He is driving a pay-as-you-enter bus.

Index

boat 8, 14, 15, 16, 19
bus 2, 4, 5, 6, 8, 10, 12, 14, 15, 17, 18, 20, 22, 23
   driver 2, 4, 18, 22, 23
   helping bus drivers 22
   facts about bus drivers 23

cash tray 4

fares 4, 5, 21

garage 2, 16, 18, 23

identity card 3

lost property 15, 16, 19

module 4, 5

passengers 8, 10, 13, 22

route 2, 7, 16, 20, 23
   plan your own bus route 20-21

seat 9, 11, 12, 22

stop 8, 10, 13, 20, 21, 22

ticket 4, 9, 23
   machine 4, 5

© 1997 Franklin Watts

Franklin Watts
96 Leonard Street
London
EC2A 4RH

Franklin Watts Australia
14 Mars Road
Lane Cove
NSW 2066

UK ISBN: 0 7496 2617 8

Dewey Decimal Classification Number: 388.3

10 9 8 7 6 5 4 3 2 1

A CIP catalogue record for this book is available from the British Library.

Printed in Malaysia

Editor: Sarah Ridley
Designer: Kirstie Billingham
Photographer: Harry Cory-Wright
Illustrations: Kim Woolley

With thanks to: Winston Jones and his son, Millie Daniel, Joan Murray-Brown, Ellie and Ben Hodgson, Mr Vic Hornblow, Mr Ray Loraine and London United Busways Ltd.

SOUTHCOATES PRIMARY SCHOOL
SOUTHCOATES LANE
HULL
HU9 3TW